Sister
Invention

**Sister
Invention**
Judith Kazantzis

Published 2014 by
Smokestack Books
PO Box 408, Middlesbrough TS5 6WA
e-mail: info@smokestack-books.co.uk
www.smokestack-books.co.uk

ISBN 978-0-9575747-8-6

Middlesbrough
moving forward

Smokestack Books is represented
by Inpress Ltd
www.inpressbooks.co.uk

To Miranda,
Lily and Irving.

Contents

PART III

PART IV

Part I

Sister invention

The mountain has the skin of a snake,
  blue and green and glowing,
flowing downwards, grasping what
  or who she's caught in her breath
until she sheds and runs at the sea.

The ladder is a phantasm, ivory steps
  you sketch in a trice on paper.
But you are there and so you must feign:
  rosy rivets, arches, shafts,
gems: tourmaline and toffee agate.

The posted signs sigh, no hooks, crutches,
  ride your white horse, rings on your toes
with cowbells on your cold, cold fingers
  to the cross of the land
where whirlwinds keep the rattling gates.

How the lift goes up and down
  touching between howling floors:
lingerie, double boilers, lad lit, chick lit
  paradise flowers, cream curtains
madam inviting your little ringed fingers.

Oh but the horse steps up the amber stair
  for she is your sister
the horse of the see-through stairs,
  the jingling bridle in the naked hand.
And you? Her constant sister of invention.

In Rome

My dear, you renew your life too often...
Te qui odi et amo...

When you are ill
          the great halls of tapestry
remember themselves quickly as bland, expert
with the muscled bodies of that trance,
          silent and sensuous, by torture
at the fingers of white-muscled executioners,

and they rifle the metal hall of night,
and they sight the slow golden morning.

Autumn is here. Don't the men sit still and write
          of the plough and the earth,
of country women with the fruitful, high-held baskets?
Let us praise the poets and their conventions.

When you are well
                    the voluminous apricot folds
of the laundered skirts and the
crisp transparent fichu, the new turban
of the Sybil, or any woman you may like

better, sailing on the Sistine ceiling, conferring
          as fresh as a practical woman,
a prospering merchant of some ways and means,
brings back the success of fruit and peaceful light:
          considerate, clever,
conversation cocked to her neighbour.

No gilded lily, but given over to your fate
comfortable, conscious of the sun

sufficient, gold for today. In her fold pocket
　　　　there hugs a death by air
and such racks, and then all the glorious what ifs —
well buried, like a hoop of house-keys,
　　　in her voluminous apricot apron...

My lover's eyes

'My mistress' eyes are nothing like the sun'
    Shakespeare

My lover's eyes are rather like the sun,
    or rather, like his horses
flashing their wild eyes along the run:
    Look how he forces

or seduces the horsemanship of light upon
    the earth in hiding,
and how she turns her back upon the sun,
    or goes out riding.

Mrs Midas

You set it, I mean that ring
on my finger, and the gold raced in,
streaked in runners of sunlight,
dayglo, gold, up my finger,
           settled in.

Into my little finger, and the middle
finger and my forefinger,
my thumb of brass gold,
my hand, a coach and five
           gold horses.

All yellow out of a fire
stoked up in one whirl, one ring.
I never noticed how the streaks
flew in, crawled in, of metal
           going cold.

Now my yellow hand is
all yours to hold in bed,
the one that strokes you heavily
where you like it, so cold,
           my honey.

Home leave

The war raged on. Then there you were.
I showed you what I'd found, the roofless
blacks, powers of greys, retirements of blue,

the walk of high walls, towers,
what was left — ashy, fire-sooted yellows,
scarlets hunched in shadows,

mansions behind whose blind eyelids
a society of women, their hands holding
opened, singed books, alarmed you,

caressed you in your red arrival
your irritable horse, your magic helmet,
asked you to stop talking, listen.

Dr Morreau's Island, the credits

Lionman... Bullman... Tigerman... Stuntman

Once the stunts lived happily
in free fall, their natural habitat.
Stunts once ranged from Everest
to the creak of the Java Trench.
They dropped through Etna to
the Astheno lakes, grazing flame,
their long tongues as quick to
the lighter flares as to the
bubbly molasseic smoulders.
In courtship stunts whirled once
on cumulous cloud banks rearing
high over the Caribbean. They
nursed their young on the Rockies
and when adult made the
customary graceful leap to the
Himalayas. Preparing for free fall
young stunts surfed avalanches,
they rode for the biggest with
almost obsessive technical joy.
In age they retired
to the eye of the hurricane
climbing its thunderous wall
into the stunts' burial chamber,
where the soul rows up
to a peep of the endless hurtling dance.

After Morreau's inept knife
the stunts, losing their wings
but gaining a syllable,
tried falteringly dropping
from cars in Bullitt chases,
diving off horses, pushing through
squares of singed bubblewrap
in designed towers,
jumping off cliffs.

In the hard skull of a stunt
fall forever angels.

The racing peacock

As a professional sprinter
the peacock scurried as fast as it could
round the burning orange marathon.
Then the bird began to falter, and slowed.
Angrily I shouted.
But the floaty plumes
rocked to a stop.
What a fiasco.
I called in the doctor.
Over the doctor's hand
hung two halves of the foot,
broken, the peacock's foot.
'Though it will heal and walk,' he said,
'this peacock will never race again.'

Mr and Mrs Blake

In my garden home
sit Adam and Eve, without leaves.
Mr and Mrs Blake are drinking tea.

In my drawing room
the wolves and the tigers roam,
the lion makes his desart throne.

But in my bedroom
he lies down with the lamb,
the curly headed woman and the man.

Mrs Blake's poem

There now, elements of pain and rage,
and beauty, got stuck in his throat

Long long ago
the lion lay down with me
under the palm-tree in the garden

His sturdy meaty lamb,
I pulled the beauty
like stringy old beans out of his sore throat
line by line
There now, like — a red flannel!

He laughed at me
flung the flannel dramatically
into the lavender
I discreetly skipped out of the way
as it were, into the shady fold
of the page

How we loved our garden.

Wintertime

Mrs Demeter how are we feeling today?
her mouth drops open
she's a hole in the ground
she's a mole
and she hisses, my spade
she's lost the spade
I lift her wrist

Don't take my temperature, it's freezing
touch my hand if you must,
cold wind sizzles off it

Dear, you're a little impatient
patience is a virtue
She'll be stuck here forever
with that fixed hole for a mouth
all the pills in the world, and she howls —

You don't know, you don't care
She was buried alive
and I wait
holed up in this hole of a place
for the grass
If I could hear the cuckoo
if green leaves cry flower,
if snowdrop and windflower the spinneys,
the verdant long-shadowed trees
If she's dead,
the unyielding moon.

Grant us a friendly smile
dear, if I was to tell you the nice news
she phoned in
this very early dawn
I was at my station
you were asleep
and she's making headway in the dark
and she's coming, soon.
Dear Mrs D
we'll have tea on the lawn.

Ghosts

Helter of wind in skelter of rain,
the storm, the worst for years,
beating the tree at the top of the hill
into a whirlpool, in near dark.
My two arrived in an armoured vehicle
carrying a bushel of presents, a turkey, cheeses,
out of the length of the afternoon,
out of the twilight
where the sycamore whipped itself
into a circle of cracking twigs,
the brow of the wood a vicious circle
round and round the sunken pit
of the old disused farm pond
as if on its own farm generator,
its own voltage of gale,
in the middle of which I had waited nervously
for the coaxing glistening engine.

Hadn't they sped chatting all day
up the M3 and down the A303
and at Exeter along to lunch in a Happy Eater
with a Christian couple who wanted to talk,
not about Christ, whose name
was on every pouted lip,
have a Happy Christmas, Happy Xmas…
and had fled the unhappy couple,
squaring off into the rampant red dragons
and the ghost lorries across Bodmin Moor,
without a tremor, debating the
morose couple and their morose child
en route for somewhere in which to feel sadly
not themselves after all and exiled —

Till they got to the Goonhillie Downs —
and a dark Goon then
snickered to me in the wind,
'You, with your little rising hopes'
though all he rode once were 'the hunting downs',
where they chased deer, boar, the wild hare.
Dumb in the dark — Call a Loved One
Make Her Happy — satellite saucers huge
as the moon is stony cold and stormless and still
behind the impervious, racing overhang
and the mill race of twig and branch —
till these Lizard lands were slithered by
and my two squealed up under the tree —

Where I bobbed out, flailing my arms
towards an embrace, two embraces,
held back in the teeth of the tree,
its storm ghosts, its out-at-sea stories,
its false lights and struggling figures,
its hull, its ribs in the swell, thrown
flotsam, like the end of a tale,
as best I could,
whatever they wished, for
1 could never know, nor they of me,
but now, then, to bring my arms round each one,
each sidling, wet, black figure in the lane
to hug and to kiss, Happy Christmas.

PART II

Dick Cheyney's Garden

I   Earth

I am pressing in eyeballs
of black caviar, delicious.
They roll from the light-as-tallow
paper lanterns of airy blooms,
the premier explosions of spring.

Where does it fall, my caviar
detailed to the tousled soil
that loves to call out for more
from the hand that feeds:
my century's project?

Wealth has oiled the marked earth,
black as the clusterlets
I calculate to underload
equally, year by year,
on every stone and every thistle.

II   Path

The street, a top thoroughfare,
could have been modern Beijing,
modern anyplace, shoppers, cabs.
What, three days of headlines — only.
But then it was Africa (Kenya).
We had hardly heard of Rwanda
by 1998 — Nor had Bin Laden, come
to that. Kenya proved the prologue
as they say, to our play.
Africans died in numbers,
some Americans, of course.
Bombs against trophy buildings,
suicides, bombs under cabs —
hardly science from two miles up —
nothing new since the War to End War.
Clinton our class hick from Arkansas
returned to dust a valuable
pharmaceutical works (Sudan).
Done titting for tat, he returned to
his own parlour for succour.
Osama B Laden was not
yet the Evil One, just, someone.

III   Walking the long lawns

Where were you when?
And as for me, what did it mean,
Camelot slumped in a limousine ... ?
Well I got married. This then:
my old Greek mother in law
fat as a baby cello, how she loved to
wash and hang my two negligees,
swing them in her Ealing garden
for all the neighbours; a sign
that must have pleased her
of the one sacral night her son
had spent with me in the Savoy
— we couldn't afford two nights.
The Greek honeymoon brought
in our summer: the white island
monastery, the blue Aegean dappling,
fishing for my lust against the eaves
                    ... later.

And later, where were you?
Coming down muzzy-headed,
What're you talking about,
tunnel, crash, night-time, her?
Who do you mean? But I knew.
I'd always backed that rich, wistful
eject: coquettish rambling rose,
spat on by the toad husband,
the toads in law, for his fault,
not hers, just like the world over.
No wonder Dodi seemed a warm arm,
that driver merely her usual fate, with
the crows on motorbikes vulturing
through the glass of the limousine
                her dying face.

And where then four years later?
At home, phoning to Dallas
of all strange circles? To Zoe:
chatting about her children:
'Judith, there's a plane crashed into'
'No it can't be true'
'I'll ring you later'

Thousands of miles east
I switch on. Toy puffs blow Meccano planes
into Lego buildings, like the Spitfires
my little brothers used to circle
like wasps over the red carpet, bang, bang.
You couldn't wring from the box more
than the voice knew, that sequence all day,
as modern transport scored its third,
and for all time, we were told, assured,
legislated to believe: The world intuned,
the times awry
                    and nature out of it.

Later I phoned Zoe's dad yourself
in your hideout in Key West, your birthday!!
Many Happy Returns Darling! Oh lord.
Unlegislated, angry, you say, I know
what it means. Afghan widows knew soon
and soon Iraq. In return:
                    Madrid, Bali, London.

Today's news is more of today,
more shells and more shivering screaming
and blood anywhere but *this* garden lawn,
'securing the sector' against 'insurgents'.
Also my right to say, not in my name?
to say, what does it mean what does it mean
what does it mean what does it mean What
                    shall we make it mean?

IV   Terror in the honeysuckle

Right at the bottom
of the very heart of liberty
lies B in his frozen lake.
Pinioned into ice,
admire his Arnie Schwarzeneggar limbs.
Wriggly as the devil, he fakes
the chocolate heart
on the pinstripe sleeve
transparently permafrost,
O Secretary of Ultima Thule.

When the Joker leads the pack,
the pack grows a hundred eyes.
It divides into fighters and drones
and hunts the Terror
right down at the bottom of our hearts.

Along the purring lane
comes Bumsfeld in his pussiline car,
he has the chauffeur pause
before invading Iraq, and stops to gaze
benignly over the right hand hedge,
counting in values of honeysuckle,

'See aft, my fat friend Ariel
puts a blindfold round the globe
or anyway the West Bank —
a fine example of our projected Garden.
However after such effort,
my mountainous friend, forever
of Sabra, Shatila, Jenin, Gaza,
will fall, sadly,
into the sleep of the Sleeping Beauty,
enclosed by the very security briar
he built for us all
against the Terror, see above:
Though who knows, it may hide right
there at the bottom of that field.'

Ahead in the mist tinted cavalcade
the Joker jams a finger
like a long hunting rifle
into the chauffeur's eye and
goes Bang Bang. The chauffeur
runs over a village. The J doubles up
with restrained celebrity joy.

A favoured child
was Bumsfeld long ago —
he would sit in the temple
among the bankers
and learned indicators
and also later he learned which
poisoned, castrated,
lamed, tongue-tied cat
could be got,
right at the bottom of its rage,
to scratch deepest.

V   Trash heap

Then I was sick — They shouted.
          They were yanking strips off me.
Then they answered the phone.
          Pukka Sahibs, my dad liked to mock.
I knew the language, how else?

Whoever was on the other end
was telling them what to ask,
Details about me and my wife —
          I was ashamed, I began sobbing.
My Britishness has a value.
          I learned a man is fair for all that.

My body is neither fair, it's dark —
I took my Citizenship Exam
— nor fair, the scars spider —
with flying colours, in harmony
— a jeer of webs across me —
          Webs of lying, lying.

VI   Gravel

Dark blue-coated inscrutable!
Dimly from the rose garden
comes the dark little cheering
for the signal of the loss of America.
But the garden is trashed
and carted away in weeds
— *our flower, our Century*

Out of the back entrance,
across a diminished gravel,
a black-gloved pallor
wheelchairs into and beyond
the windows of darkness,
briefly rolled down,
then shrouded again
now that his aching frame —

I have tired it, even abused it
for you, America ingrate —

now that his shoulders,
constructed for the world's weight,
have been ensconced with tender care
by his knights, the teary staffers.

And he waves, the glove shiny, well made.
The driver turns the key into night.
O Bucephalus, O Alexander.

You can say you saw a smile
hurt as only the broad sun
can shine in a malign winter.

My simile — your responsibility.
So don't blame me.

I may come again, America.

Any old iron

Now the child in the bedroom
has roses on a blue trellis
she chose for herself,
to hide from the fierce grownups,
and the barges hoot down the river
in the early mist.

Now she has become a backer
of complex metals,
a taxpayer of drones
hovering over other trellised streets
trundling highend wares
from sky to house to child.

The old cry advanced, retired,
the pony walked
rough London and smart London
dragging the cart:
Bring out your saucepans and kettles,
bring out your past.

In the early morning,
sometimes the totter,
cigarette, clothcap. I lean out,
hear him call above the trit trot,
standing on the piled junk, Any old —
bicycles, bits and bobs, fridges.

Last of the old cries, he fades
and day comes and supper,
then the sleep among monsters
partying the night, and the clouds
orange tipped, aglow like cigarettes
above the rooftops, then thunder

gallops in over mountains, and a crying
rises and wanders
down the piled up streets.

Curers

What butchers know is how to deal
the last cut, unfreeze even a dead ham.
They are the helpers of the street, the
carers, but they can't turn a weathered cheek.

Cross customers are curses to slaughterers,
feeding their panic of being all alone,
fighting, fighting in the locked up deep
frozen chest of meat and not touching.

So they reach out with stubby thumbs,
turning the queue into statues where
we stand, smiling good thank you thank you
we're better now oh we're prime.

Capture Rapture

We've rescued the Garden of Eden,
took it back. God is blessed,
the terrors of the Enemy
to be expected. He loved those
apples, plums, nectarines, peaches.
The juices hissed down his dark hide.
They suppurated in the sacred rivers.
So we sat down and smoked by the waters.
We cleansed the apples and peaches.
We oiled them to such a bloom.
This for me was our great triumph.
The armoured vehicles alone used
more than a million gallons of oil
each day. We can see further.
From Samara to Naja. The first
serious resistance. We killed about 100,
imagine! the miracle of thermal imaging.
Then, a trial, the worst sand storm
for twenty years. The Garden receded
into the deluge. We pushed on.
Bravo 1 and Bravo 2 were buried —
they went up in flames. Bravo, brothers!
We got him out alive, decorated by fire.
The flaming sword. The Fallen One.
We were getting confused. Genesis
whirred and stuck in a dust djinn.
But in the end the Abrahams
tanks rolled into the oasis. Where Allah
lay burnt out as a little newborn child.
(What travesty! But we weren't
that confused). We swaggered
on the enormous returning troop-carrier,
we laid it on the marble steps,
by the four corners, red-spotted,
we had tramped the dusty roads,

bundle over our shoulder, just a hobo
like from the poorest backyard.
Then God said: Shucks and Aw!
And we cheered and opened
our pocket handkerchief and
spread Allah, crisp as a fall bonfire,
at His long extensive toes.

Who loved me

One night — I'm eight, one of those little girls
in love with ponies, and also Jesus the brown-eyed —
I'm in bed and dreaming at random.
Why was it Red, the Sea? The innocents,
chestnuts, bright bays with four white stockings,
plunging, their soft mouths on fire,
the charioteers whipping their flanks
desperate for land. The two wave wings
clap together —

And now, open all hours,
later and later into the night.
He drowns horses Who loves me.

The sea is a thick red tongue
lapping from the arteries of Iraq.
All day it lubricates, it refills
the pumping heartlands where I live.
No wonder at night the heart shudders.
What flesh, what life it flushes down
from Falluja, Baghdad, Basra,
the drained hearts, no tougher than
the beasts I drove crazy out to sea that night,
before in their radiance
they pranced into the thunder:

prayer to old Brown Eyes at bedtime,
from the white-ribboned girl for her pony;
for all things sunny, healthy,
huge, the appetite for life.

The bombed woman

All the times the screaming head,
the bombed woman,
sees the planes about to
sees her town, her children, herself.
All those times
inside this skull
out through this mouth
sorrow's grinding scream
protrudes its lava
of terror, knowledge.
This organ plays a march
unstopping, never composed.
The backing is gray flesh —
not wind, brass or string —
the discords silent.

The viewing listening person,
the reading listening viewing person
shouts, calls with all heart
to the sorrow of the bone heap.
But heart flutes down to a peep —
Who can quaver Stop?
The enemy has come, flesh screams.

But the enemy has also gone:
Stop, the heart whines,
Don't you see, mouth,
something dreadful,
I have to stop these raids,
we are upside down now,
I am the bombed woman.
You are the plane,
humming, droning, tearing
the snowy countryside
into furrows. Your shells
are coffins I can't bear.

Finally for a while
I watched her close her scream
not because I'd calmed the world.
Only, all are dead and here I am.

Praise for the head

Ariel Sharon, murderer of untold thousands of Palestinians,
died in 2014 after eight years in a coma.

May I introduce
the Prime Minister,
sage of the belly,
one of us,
warrior king for the emptied land of kings
where he plants his feet,
concrete and polished facts on the ground
straddling the sea
of terrorists and little girls with satchels.

Whoever speaks evil
against that aged man
and his top of white hair,
they'll see no evil —
their eye irises
indefinitely detained —
Nor hear evil —
hobbling along in
eyemasks, earmuffs, mouthtapes.

The animals are eyeless in cages,
You stacked the little girls in towns
You stalled the small boys inside a wall
concrete as the wonderful world around us.
May the sky shower down
candies and cookies
over your tireless head.

*

In this way we all saw the head
of that aged man, General Ariel Sharon,
as a light bulb, the day of days, continuous.
Babel head. Lit up the sky. Such gratitude.

Could not imagine the following:
Popped dead, stopped dead, propped up:
head suddenly out on its own
in out in out
day by day.

What does the head dream?
Beyond even his one bad dream,
the tremor he immediately forgot
after the first act,
the long smear on the hands
so long ago.

Rockets are the jokes of the weak

Gaza, 2008-9

The jokes land in ploughed fields
or bash into a wall or two.
Laughing so hard killed one soldier
in a year and wounded several civilians.
Still, fun in the wheat,
whistling over a closed border,
a blockade and a siege to boot,
we were not amused.

Finally we couldn't resist.
Unable to stifle our own
more democratic laughter,
and ever eager to impart our
more civilized sense of fun,
we ran a hilarious sitcom
over three weeks
for 1400 Gazans.

What a show!
They fell over laughing.
They crawled, howling. No surprise.
We have perfect timing, delivery,
state of the art material.
See what happens to clumsy jokes
about the birth town
of the Minister of Defence.

Child in Gaza

Gaza, 2008-9

I was a little child
born in the Gaza ruins.
My name was Palestinian
and my heart was strong.

On the Israeli green
the little children played,
I asked to share the play
and they sent back fire.

Why did they send white fire
that melted away my flesh?
They said it was the gift
my jealousy required.

Why did they burn me so?
In white bandages I die
in a hospital like a ruin.
Remember, what I know.

On Terror

Crunched behind a bush
30 metres back, he hoists
the blind-fire rocket,
all he's got.

Watches the drones coming
steadily in steel droves,
automated sheep skipping
high over the wire —

Up and just about over —
Headfirst it ploughs a field.
Back a bit, the wolves press the buttons
of the sheep, and drink coffee.

He squirms home at night.
Rearms from a small cache.
Terror in a cellar...
On return they glide and dock in hangars.

Bin Laden in the Gulf of Iran

By the time he reached the bottom
of the Gulf, by the time
on the way down, half a
mile you thought, two and a
half thousand feet, neither
of us could make out metres of
metres of metres, hours then,
even the humble seconds
that lowered the slightly
smiling lips, the bedraggled
infested prophet's beard past
creatures zoologists can name,
not I, smaller and smaller
his own citizens, denizens,
his followers, who came with him
devoted, from the worshipped
land, the cause, to the end of it,
erupting all along the passage down,
in, or out, moving from their
accustomed cells through or to
other cells, all intent on eating, him,
each other; propagating, changing,
swimming, dying in the depths they
did not anticipate, he after all a mere
land animal like the other animals
who shot him and tipped him
into the only element he could not
claim for his soul or his god.
Bits of him fly like rag flags
on battlements of coral —
in full fathom — what was it?
Failing metres, we didn't know
that either. Wrong. Not the math,
but his (I grant you) efficient
unmartyrdom. Wrong: he

should have lived but in murder's
lock; and his drowners,
so should they, for great murders
that came in revenge, and come
and come, and slaughter has two roads,
two songs sounding off,
and the saints go murdering on.

Every march I make

Julia, I swear I take your number
every march we meet
Palestine, Peace, Afghanistan, Iraq.

Everything in my pocket
ends up shredded. Why's
my memory at war?

I heard your voice. Will I
shout out then: I know your face,
the day before this street is closed?

What we did in the holidays

Some of us, rightly or wrongly, thought that the town
    had seen things it shouldn't,
we may have exaggerated the smell, the sweetish smell
    that crept up through the floor
of the kitchens. We suddenly wondered if we were baking
    our own thighs, oblivious, I mean,
still on in our stoves. At that point, nauseated, we felt we
    should drive to the seaside
to catch pure air, our ozone gift, our toffee brown seaweed,
    our miniature life forms,
delicacies delectable and quaint in the fingernail tide pools.

Sunset off Key West

I swore a hill city
with people standing all over it waving
glided beyond the spider web

but you said
it was the biggest cruise ship in the world
crawling the moving branches,
soundlessly along the channel.

I swore a great black insect
perched on the horizon, extending
the bowed laundry lines of its wings
to dry at the sun's boiler.

But you said
it was a shrimper plying in to Safe
Harbour after two days out
and offering up its big nets to dry.

Then an osprey snatched a
great sea bass out of the channel
hissing by land's end;
the bass dangled and wagged
in its claws, then a bald eagle
dove from the sun and fought the osprey
till the fat fish dropped down
into the closing waves and the fighters
rushed east screaming over the wood.

But you said
it was a plane joy-riding
over the round heads of the swimmers,
towing behind its long transparent tail
FORTY-FIVE DOLLARS ROUND TRIP FOR TWO
SEE PARADISE FROM THE AIR
Then it dropped white leaflets
onto the beach and soggily into the waves.
And like an oldfashioned sun
the red-haired face of the Ranger
wheeled out of the wood,
his fast walkie-talkie wagging
in his freckled grip.

And we could not see:
not hill city nor insect,
bird nor fish, there was
such a light, such a dazzle.

But you swore it was the sun,
oldfashioned, with red
equilateral flames
spitting down behind the weed trees
and shining so loudly,
guttering with such orchestral,
voluminous might,
we could not hear another sight,
nor see another word we said.

The dose

After a night dose of rain,
a steam noses up to the window,

the mangroves, ferns, sea grapes,
like a faint skunk whiff

— distinct from the damp earth after rain,
the rain I was born to, how it

sprang down to my greeting or I would run
with it on my eyelids, drop by drop

during each cloud's downpour;
then we would say, O rain, get to Spain

or those southern parts that really need it —
But here… is this smell

stealing along my path
like a sickbed stranger out of the stinking woods.

Alligator

Notice the evening sky getting stormy
and blue behind the big people's house,
the big house with toy blue shutters
so closed against burglarisation.
My head drips so from the canals
I admit I'm almost ashamed to stare.

Last night in the cold air of a front
their alarm screamed off as the wind banged
on the shutters. The house burst
into a creaking, the shutters sprang open
and for a time from my starry recline
on the lawn bank, I saw them stand stiff

like bristling hair, then snap to.
That's why I try to avoid the stare
of the house fixing at me between
those jalousies. The people are away
but that house is trained to handle a gun.
One day poochie pooch will run out to play.

Four walls

As soon as the wind,
like a tuning finger,
like the jerky arm on an old record player
swings back again and then again,
like a discreet peep to a trumpet,
raised to the wide poised lips
in the larger dive next door
whose space we had forgotten until
it began to spread once more, four walls of wind,
(now the wind inflates, now blows
right into our own living-room, this audioed air:
neither click, cursor nor mouse can switch it down
nor quiet our house or soothe the palm-trees).
As soon as the wind comes

taking me by the scalp, spilling,
rising and dying in and out of my sockets,
holding me up by my ears, as if I'm merely
the black garden snake, the red-collared one
that licks like a bootlace across the path,
liking the winter sun, and then hides
beneath the five aged palms clashing
in the moonless salty dark.
As soon as the wind comes,

turning out the pockets of the house,
the gum-chewing leader steps up,
wipes his mouth, raises the trumpet
take it away John, Charlie, Echo Bravo Charlie:
all night it swings, all night,
and beyond, the tugs of the cruise liners
(Ecstasy, Aphrodite, Majesty, Inspiration)
woo and woo hugely on arrival/departure
to/from our poor damn lump of marl
for its sins named Earthly Delights:
'Stuff me fuck me do me' — the tees on Duval Street,
and the Disney street train for the older obese —
But as soon as the gale comes,

when it cruises into its loud berth
it buries the tees under the five thrashing
Washingtonia palms. A waste site, absentminded,
encrypted in mounds of fish bones, oyster shells:
hearth snakes, a nattering of voices in the fronds
prophesying in turn to the ocean and the gulf,
not so much war as these night invasions,
pale countries whose passwords
melt and change in the air. Every two minutes
a giant invasion fades away,
a new rises and passes, no spy
could sort this out, such soundless
discord, dissonance, harmonies
over the hair of my head as the moon slowly climbs.

To Zion, Utah

We come to the other side,
enormous and tawny. I tell you
we have found heaven. We fly right in.

The river moves through the peaks
of the divinities forgotten, absent
or missing. I'm sure we can find them.

They've gone for a walk
up the pearly slick rock, two hundred
million years ago (before dinosaurs).

Dominations and powers,
triumphs, seraphim and cherubim
in all their glory, why were they

so stranded, way too late on in their lives.
They had swung high then low.
Beneath their flight the canyons

sprayed like pressed foliage,
the myriad unfalling winters of skeletal leaves —
manna drifts on the desert.

Faces pressing, peering down: the window
harks the apostate angels' song —
O rapturous into Zion!

Canyon

Recent evenings at the red-gold mountain,
eroded hand swaying on a stick,
ingrown as a dogtooth,
a woman stands,
wind, rain, snow wrenched from the buttress.

Saying to me — without the shadow
of a look, so how does she know me:
'Go on in...' Like skin
a door is printed on the brown tortoiseshell
cliff face; but it hasn't a handle.

She takes out her eye from her head
and clamps it onto the stone.
The alarmed watery eye gives a blink.
It swivels round to the left
It looks round painstakingly to the right.

Pointing her forefinger, trembling,
cocked up over the bone of her long stick,
she enters the stone.
The brimming eye turns round on me.
But every evening now, the dark shuts my own.

---

*In the Navaho creation story, Spider Grandmother
lives in the Canyon du Chelly, Arizona*

PART III

Easter Monday

Above my favourite ever race-track
the clouds in their white silks
chase one another in the gallops of the blue sky:
quarter horses and riding ponies,

herding, pulling apart without a squeal,
circus ponies, shires, all classes of crest,
flank and hindquarter, nose to nose
nudging over the laps of the downs.

But none of us care about the weather:
we work our eyes, brains, on the alluring odds
and at last on that single irreversible
all for all and glory of the pell-mell

on which I could stake in a single moment
even my own nags, the ambling downs themselves,
barely shedding their patched winter coats,
scrappy velvet under the new spring.

Plumpton Races, Plumpton Green. Sit,
uncertain ramrod on a folding chair,
airing my odds as they drift in from the cold,
heavy going and easy going and

inland over this green soft-going round,
summer, autumn, winter and now spring.
Check halfway, confirm the coloured dots
strung flat out on the tilted plain,

Hardy Breeze, Northern Saddler, Nearly Gold,
and overhead, in their opposite career,
never jibbing but changing, the chances
even and even along the blue plain.

Owl

Not a paper ghost   nor a beating kite
lifting before a groundswell   the way they all say
white low in the falling sun out of a block of woods
then powerful in concentration   great milk white face
narrow eyes   sombre along furrows
                    wing sweeps
                                no sound   out of my sight

The meadows were pure bedlam next time   the sun lay
over the roast lambs   sinking lazy   timer rings   pretty in
the evening little lambs we eat thee   no longer cute but
stout   but still crying like quite contrary   cockleshells
all in a flock   for mothers long gone   the river long gone
in the dark of alders and scrambling willows   the long
white arm of the pretty teenager upslung over the bough
she hangs over the punt and the pool   daddy come quick
(giggles in the gloam)   I'm going to fall   help!
shouts splashing of oars and fools   the moon will be up
as white as her flung arm   and the sun will take itself
behind the downs   the lambs will lie down in sleepy
circles without the bulky mothers   done roamin
wolves no more than old twitches in the night

Come out to please a tired walker   my eyes
being good for nothing but roosting crows   will you
come out in a circle   will you
            coast the world?
                        beating   hushing
        here   there
                    now   sometime

Hopkins Skipkins

I

Why not with glory to
  a morning's life,
joints, ligaments, muscles,
muscles, ligaments, joints —
   Stilted, stale, salty
as a pork pie on the shelf
  stiffened in the window
  where the replete go by.

  Glory to this morning,
    baffled on tippitoe,
its bottly hop, its baby joy.
  Did I wake up fettered?
Who was it jumped, shocking foe,
   blundering in the night?
I was in the outsider's way.

Glory to my scurfy struggles,
  daily like the butcher's bang
   I would, I couldn't pay,
If I can join the shiny aconite
    after a snail of Sundays
  in their separate slimy land:
the butcher's continent, the land
of throat cut by the counterpane —

When with gales carving up the house,
  I was tripe and offal on the tray,
    what did I dream?
    The outside was less
      than the inside.
Spring spent fast and half the summer,
   dizzy as the dim red hen
    corkscrewing down —

Dreams! What dreams does a hen falling
dream? Cleaver's terror?
That's how the outside world upends her
and pity rears its crest,
grotesquerie —
Glory to the hen for hanging on!
I sing her yellow scaly legs and
also her talons.
Up on the crossbeam she scrabbles —

Glory be to all of us for life
(though upside down like bats
asleep in the barn,
the cave
with not a form outside
or beyond) —

Like grim death,
for lunch I munch
the wondrous formless fruit of glory.
I hang around
for dear life
I have such tenderness —
to sing good health to all my scarpered bills.

II

O day deliveranos

They tear my hair out all night.
    Short and coarse, the hair
of the woman whose long teeth
        have nothing to do
    but to gnaw her all night,
 pecata mundi all night long

O day deliveranos

He chews the pockets of his head
where memory bleeds from a sore gum
inflamed still by its baby teeth,
points which never smoothe.

From the craters of the night
O day deliver the lot of us,
the baby sewn into mud;
how grown souls spring up at night

and stamp around their ruins.
May anger hunch to a lost turning,
a pinch of injured spite on the map I left
in a black ditch of frogs.

    O day and wind deliver us
from the red gasp in your throat,
O light of the mind of the morning
        receive my breath.

III

Shall I be healthy, shall I be
healthy? Happy may do
as it please. All I ever wanted
was a
   a little bit of butter
            for my bread.

O little stolen slice of life
on a mouthy brown bread crust
hot from the racked oven.
Hail to the lusty lamb
that having nuzzled life
runs along the sunken lane
under the bled sky,
graven trees,
and for its sunset
hops among
a glory of pots and pans
set on the clown-coloured flame.

Flock

Wavery
in the water glass
of the leafy elder,

to, fro,
titmice in a shiphold.
None to be twitched,

snatched, shot
by lens, hawk
or the orange cat.

Kensal Green Cemetery

I sat on a black vault slab
    carved Wyndham Lewis,
        watching a big black crow
           that sat above me.

I knew her prim old caw
    said nothing to me
        but warned Wyndham Lewis
        I sat upon him.

Braziers

On my bag or heart I sewed
pearl button swirls swearing Love,
and where are they so sweet and hard won —
Surely not gone. Velcroed loves:
casually, a coat torn on a fence.

Take pearls white from the sea;
but the sea at the end of this valley
is grey-brown, kicks green all winter,
no pearls. New buttons, even so…
and how manage with such baby threads?

Old buttons roll into their holes.
Still, whether been and gone, it seems
they're wired in for life, a look,
a conversation on a corner,
the match flare of a thrilled smile,

that one brighter than the sunset
has stirred our day's porridge of cirrus.
A dagger sky, dragon red, green,
the braziers exploding quietly to nothing.
Good friends, friends, the blue dusk.

The twilight house

Slow loris in the London Zoo,
why look at me so?
Your spectacles are hugely disproportionate,
puddles of thought.

What blue moonlight to see me in,
much better than I see you.
You slouch your
naked constructed branch.

Across the black alley
hurls the fast loris. She moves
round, round and round her cage
and never finds rest.

Rat mistresses of little night,
tail me back to the house
where the women in the black cloths
stare at my legs. How thick the legs

rush and curtsey-stumble past them daily,
sorry Mother, morning Mother,
late white loris for Math, English,
Religious Education. How serene

in time, slow slow and round,
to trip any child on the make,
to dim any reasonable light that
might visit the house where they

had us in rows, room by room.
I chased nothing at all,
it turned out, but their great hope,
in their rodent's gnawing

nocturne, the veil, the fallen vale
they said was human life —
their great hope I mean in death:
death that tries to trip up the stairs to light.

Wolfchild

You sheltered yourself from the damp
in a red hood and a red raincoat,
You were, even, timid in the dark wood
backing from a sudden tee-hee.
You hated that masquerade of
the drowned child, that knowing
wolfish child who chased you whining
over endless watery bridges.

What could you do but keep
your head down, soft face averted,
(a lure as it was to kiss) stern or hurt?
By the mere twitch of a delicate lip
you gave the news not to the world
but to me. Am I not the wolf?
Small, bad, I sneak up — Look:
lying down, crossing my forelegs,
I am Christ the lamb at your feet,
let me be merciful, little alma mater.

Blessed Agnes

The church was old, the bishop older,
the small girls were uniformed,
they never giggled, for fear of hell
— felt fear, stalking the back alleys of the mind.

No one told them otherwise. So it was:
contrary to schoolgirl lore, comic, poetic,
pornographic, cinematic. So it was.
We wore our cheap net veils

and put on shy/sly faces. We filed.
We each had picked our Confirmation Name:
It had to be a saint of course, but
classier to pick a red robed Martyr.

Naturally afire to affirm
self-sacrifice and modest heroism,
I plumped for Blessed Agnes,
a thirteen year old Roman virgin,

a noble enthusiastic convert to the Lord.
Refusing her suitor, brave Agnes prayed
instead to meet the smelly roaring lions
before the smelly roaring crowds —

Though thanks to a cruelly
influential dad her stardom was denied —
she must join her neck to the axe
in her own bower. Disappointment

smiled to meet the heavenly groom.
But how I dreamed! How I was moved!
And so we moved to meet the bishop's
old grey thumb; it scraped its oily crosses.

Silence, little girls: a dozen more
axed souls are delivered! Afterwards
we played hopscotch. I'm sure of it.
As for the bishop, that mirage of stern

embroideries, only the high vendor of God,
his shiny heaven and his bootblack hell,
could have thumbed my Agnes
out of her bloody bower, told her to run along.

The well bespoke

'intrinsically disordered'
                    Pope Benedict XVI on homosexuality

Forgive a soft spot for such shoes
inside out of crimson silk,
a silk that Prada specified
of silkworms putti plump on virgin milk,

then dyed to match that matchless blood
whose wounded steps my little feet,
they do say elegantly formed,
thus imitate to trip downstairs and greet

the boring nuns and clever gentlemen
for whom I wave my little wave.
Blood-red beauty! These are the shoes
in which infallibly we trip to save.

Eternal and cigar

for my brother Paddy, 8 June 2005

You were the life and soul, how could
  you leave so soon? Paddy dear,
 no more crowing? Just a sister clucking
for a gone beyond recall old cock?
  Left with this nightly tipple of not —
till I burn the same hole in zero.

Paddy, it's so easy, in drab sadness,
  to take your best wit in vain.
 Don't mind me, and I won't mind me.
I'm looking and looking: sugar and heaven
  deprived, with my unbelief's
worn out gnashers. Only hard fudge

left for the old bag... stones on the stomach.
  Didn't I crave the same perfect glory,
 the enchanted tiers, the overhead lightning —
and of course the very best pork pies to come —
  Heart and soul on a pure drift,
your rich traditional bellow the best speeches

we ever had (in ever-heckled congratulations
  of big birthdays of special saints,
 mother, father, lost too, darling and dear) —
which soon so crack up all your greeting saints,
  they flap off their fluffy banquettes
and in a rustling rush flip-flop feet together

back to chaos, back into shoes, into their own
  sitting-rooms, bedrooms, bathrooms,
 into traffic jams, bars, pubs, betting-shops,
and the last time I saw you, a June Friday,
  cutting an enormous cigar,
tenderly, behind the door, as I said goodbye.

Stephen's Day

Now comes a warhorse,
white muzzled,
saddled with crimes,
my robin's a' flying

my robin's the dark one

Hallooed, hunted
on the day of Stephen,
died in the winter hail,
quiver to arrow

my robin's the dark one

arrow to breast,
blood's wound.
move earth, come sun
light armoured

my robin's the dark one

Toads and diamonds

This story concerns the toads:
who glisten too, and what's more, they live.
They pour out of her witty mouth,
too caustic for a good woman,
and down they bound
between two lusciously moistly
reprehensible breasts,
and leap out and are lost
in the green of the forest.
All but one, the smallest, the wickedest
at heart, hardly more than a quark
or that maritime particle I will
never see on the waves or the
bridge of her or your nose — unseen,
unseeable. Anyway, tossed out,
it wanted damp, not the ocean,
just a toad's damp. It crawled
from her lip, up, straddling
the chimney of nose and cheek,
the new land still not quite moist;
it sensed something at last
that in the muffled legendary forest
would have been a mere
or merely a pond (barely a puddle).
It crawled up the years of its life.

Her fine thinning hair grew silver,
done in a bun which always
broke loose and flowed like the strands
of a marsh stream. But every night
from time to time her hand brushed at a fly
on her cheek, a fly on her nose
in her sleep. At last the poor dried beast
hardly alive, eased its desperate breathing
like a bag across the meniscus of the mere,

rested outstretched,
webbed its wicked joints,
gently secured its sucker pads
and gratefully flumped on its pumping belly.
Cataract! they said: not to worry.

In the annals of the eye department
great doctors shot whole batteries
like marksmen — puff, puff —
at her cornea, her lens, her retina,
the grand optic nerve itself,
the causeway across the spongy forest,
fishing for news (a toad
who remained at rest, gurgitating
a strenuous past, burping its
gentle raspberries at the radiologists).

The forest is jewelled with new avenues,
glisters open, shut, open wider:
back and forth wind the neural horns:
it hurts I hurt it hurts it hurts

Coda

Could that be the pain of the damned?
the good sister teased long ago,
she who angelically without explanation
acquired the lung power one day
lost in the green of the forest
to spout like a cherub
gold, roses, diamonds, pearls, sugar and spice

The lost recalls nothing. Her brain.
She presses her hand to her diamond eye.

Fairytaleprincess tale

In her hands there sat a toad.
'How can I possibly kiss such a moist,
warty, dry, slimy creature?' Her hands
wrinkled beneath its advance,
a sucker on her pulse. 'Eech.'
She throws it back on the parapet
of her prince's pond. Tut, it is
the Prince. She clasps him in delight.

Then one day, soon after
the best TV wedding the people
had ever googled, and, it seems
without the slightest look behind,
no bother at all, prince flips
off under the water lilies. She illogic —
where should toad hide but in the
prinzpond — pleads for his silken kiss,
not this grief. Now, a shriek
and she's stepped out of the white lilies,
the royal stare of the future.

Now hop and spy the passion of
the real prince in his warty water-garden,
a toad in his hole of gold water,
one reverse flip, he's re-enthroned.
'I'll hug you between my breasts,
I'll be pregnant with little princes,
(mimicking the fat lilies on their pad),
your mother, father, everyone will be delighted.

Now will you forsake your hole
of golden water forever, my own,
my reptile?' 'Not on the cards,'
lays out the selfish beast; and
jumps back into the Bowl.

That muddy bottom bears the parade
and the jangling of martial braid,
gold as the hair of the little Princess above,
heavy layered by tears. 'But I can't live
out of the bowl of my rushes.
I'm off for my jolly old plunge,
I'll be around at breakfast'.
She throws her big bellied misery
down the palace stairs, looks up,
astonished, no harm done, he looks
down, Mum too, Dad too, the whole
toad clan squints down, their thick lids
drooped. 'Why did she do that,
hysterical girl?' Warty times pass,
threshings round the lily stems,

beyond the long ago placid months
        that went to make each
            golden-lidded little one
    long before our dropsy time when
                everything foretold is done.

Skylla

Dog heads at the end of tentacles
waving like the tails of a pack of hounds.
Pups in the womb. Abandoned. Miscarriage
re-enacting each its death
slobbering down the side of the cliff
each time there's a ship.
The echoes whimper back
what delicacy they're snatching
up out of the spitting race,
retrieving for *me*. As in former times
the sacred hounds in glamorous woods
hunted with the Goddess? I wish.
First Homer finally Ovid.
Shipmasters drown the last yells.
(Mine too, a fainter cry.)
Men Overboard!
Divided, they say at port,
between two murderous women.

Imagine a lost younger sister.
A bubble of laughter, (naiads?)
giggles, chat, long draped hair,
This the pretty hairdo scene
under the waterfall, the rocky gate
in every single heroic cliff
where every river god meets Poseidon.
But one day the tide reaches further.

Elements of a spark, doused.
A splutter in the mind's rock.
How was she? Beautiful? Gifted?
Did she laugh? Pleasant to know?

I, she, ache at waist level, hip level,
feed their canines, their baby claws.
I, they, are tearing who they live for,
all to bits, elegantly, year by year.
No longer possible to eat with that beak.
I, she, with that beak.
Translate: She who 'rends'.

It never works
For every soothing it takes
more flesh to soothe, a cushion
to flesh the anguish of stone.
The faint yelp of a puppy.

*

Poets peer, epics grow.
The dogs of the womb take for
each hero, six cheeky sailor boys,
cheeky boys for cheeky pups.
The hero skirts the yippity-yap,
the teeth far inside, cruel teeth, unsacred.

Why me, she barks, why not him?
and all those cheeky lads?
Good question, floated like paper
from one to the next tearaway.
The beautiful, evasive papers,
birch bark, papyrus, parchment, paper,
our own current translation, uniform
white, or gold, or blue (the universe?)
or all to black in the split
element of a flash, spark,
a splutter in the mind's rock.
And after a year and a day
will my voice come back to me?

But under the waterfall
really — how might she be?
Was she a beauty? Witty, quick?
Postscript: the wickedest queen,
no god's invention neater,
her crooked finger
to find the chink in little Skylla
— her job to needle —
find it open, bloody,
then stuff her back down herself
screaming, caught for good by
her first/last ocean of desire.

So that in the dark
behind the rock face
notorious to men and ships
the long hair of the waterfall
dries to snake and dog,
the zoo in the hill of the womb,
and as in all such strange cases
(O aborted women)
the misshapen begins to grow.

Labrys' child

I am the axe of two horns
well grown
           born of beast hair
and her sharp flesh

The pretty mother
        I hear tell how
             she shines
how white, how white,
        bedded like fire

Burning higher
    it climbs higher
her horned silhouette

    What is daylight?

Shine on me
    They say the day
           is white, but you
                are white —
and night is bluer,
           something bluer

and soft, Pasiphae,
           two horned mother —
Look — how these dark nights
           you are new

In your rounding lips I swell
        in you bedded I shine
             we grow fat
How these darker nights
    you grow old
        shrink from me

I carry you in my mouth
        I trot and bury it
in the curled bones of my nest

What the head sings

I

The soft marsh had been crossed twice.
The tramp home. Heart in the mouth.
To see the rising path out of the fog.

Triumphant. How easy, how more than easy
to look ahead. Delight paced the thighs
as unfamiliar, more emaciated than mist
at dawn. Rose, saffron. Whisper it.

Uphill, the air got purer. The sun
a pelt on my shoulders. And before my eyes,
a dark kiss on the path. They never thought.
What worms. My eyes are your mirrors.

So I wore you before and behind, darling
armour. And you before me were defended
by my double arms. Were we unnatural?
Not to sun and shade. Miracles all the way.

Like snowdrops — or the birds all neck to
beak I saw feed head down in the sulphur.
To such wealth, what were the steps
of two shadows. Not shade but shadow!

The birds can scream on, the sun rose.
His dark love whispered to her dark adviser
who led, head poking, nose forward.
She hung just a bit behind him.

My selves, I and dark I: two shells,
my black pearl walked between.
What was dead is found, life's proof...
I proved it, I shout: 'We're together!

We're one!' A headshake: 'Don't
stop or turn or say anything.' No need.
Forgive me everything, my excitement.

II

Black, fainter, stronger, gliding up scree.
Rivulets, ruts, paw marks, vast
avenues of human feet pouring the other way,
there wasn't a print going this way.
A long way, longer going up, much longer.

She walked before me, between me and me
— I sing you, the sun paints you —
She bent — are you falling — to pick something?
She caught, fumbled a muddle of darkness,
I couldn't see the hand, it wavered,

dappled, its fragments trickling away,
finger, thumb, black tendrils, black grapes
half dazzling, gone, remaking, breaking,
What's the ill sun doing? Rising, falling.
I felt my hot shoulders cool — 'don't turn.'

His black hand groped backwards,
disappeared, and the black flowers.
Not there. Where? Into my hair the
poke of a stalk. Ah love, shadow,
ah stalking scare shadow, tease —

So I sing of the fickle sun, then nearly
above me, and sing, dear, how it twirled,
irresponsible dancer out of the cloud.

III

She reached up with the wild
spraying hat, a moment.
The taller bent back,
let himself be crowned,

I saw her nod, silhouetted curls,
so long since I saw the curls
I kissed, mouthed, sang of —
But not an iota of a face,

not an eyelash for me. Eyeless.
We walked on past flowers
too easy on the eye.
What had they sent me?

The shadow wreathed him
a hat, yes — I slowed a stride,
impatiently watched it place the vine
on his head, all three
of us moving, the scratch
of leaves, grapes soft and swollen,
I too breathed, heard no breath behind —
Happy am I, roared the lark's song.

The hand reached forward.
His groped back. But the fingers
broke again, shimmered,
anemone over rocks,

the scattering underwater.
Fingertips... never... never touch —
Now, give up this stupidity.

IV

Hear that breath? Oh, clearly!
It bled back, frailer, gaunt,
dwindling past me, the hips, waist,
for a long time I held your/its breasts.

They were right behind, the bastards.
They always were, breaking every promise
they ever made, blind white eyes,
a wave of sulphur over rocks like jelly.

Shade, shade, come out to play —
poor little worm, to soften me up,
chaw me back down as well. We're scars
on a hard face. What a big fish am I.

The harp shivers wherever you are.
Goodbye the midday sun that stands
sheer overhead and empties the path,
Heaven and hell, shared bad nature.

Eurydice, I turn to wherever you are,
you my shadow, I yours, dear home in
any hat or headgear or wreath or wrath.
The same old dance to which we turn...

And so I'll call our tune
                    mouth to sun
Orpheus Orpheus what shall we play?

Shadows across the harp strings
                              my rainbow
This is what the head sang on the rivers.

Who am I?

I was a man who rode a ram
        by his short and curlies,
    a man almost inside a sheep.
            Who am I?

I was a man who rammed a giant tree
        into a giant's eye.
  Believe in me
      or in his giant will to die.

Wherever sea rails
        or gales fly,
   the flock patters on dusty feet.
        Everyone must eat, or die.

That eye rides glaring on my prow,
       captive now,
  protecting No Man,
        good man, every man.

Song for Matala Bay

1

Cockcrow like a delphinium spire
rounding up into blue entry.
Mountains have strung their honied
entrails here, bow-bellied
limestone by a slip sea
                        glazing stony Matala.

   In dark waters
    the town sprats play
   before dawn, their
        aquatic harpsichord.

Under window softly and hurriedly
goes a hen, a ghost
without shoes; the cock her scythe-
tailed tack-voiced paramour again
breaks brazen sound beneath hills.
An infant under the cypress
a Heracles addressing the bedrooms,
having wrestled off, he says
                        the snaky shadows.
The shutters are opened, and he prowls
at a field's distance, his head
as upright as a coin chieftain's
with few brains, in the drought stiff grass.

2

Two striped snails
climb the slanting cypress trunk
journeying to Heraklion nonstop.
Now that the sun is up
and has breathed into its disk the sky,
the streamlines of a spider
between trunk and wall
quiver in and out, now there,
now waved out of eye; pricked
in, two girders sapphire.

In incurable heat,
          the spider to its stone,
     voices hurry on the upper road

where lorries hurl
to Matala; the manager
sweats a visit on his moped
among arguing flies.
After he has gone
the pillow on the verandah
is a boulder under head.
Curlews over field
issue their thin collective chime.

3

A carload of children down
to trifle with the sea
    that glazes Matala
        town of sprat and shell.

A bed of geraniums, a whirl of sand
to tease the hermit with —
red blobs, surrounded by the hens
back from a troop march, from a bivouac
under the honied mountain
fixed by the side-eyed cock
from which he has stepped in reptile boots,
wagging his back and sides.
They argue in oily murmurs
the noon merits of geranium beds,
the quality of beetles.

And a hornet occasionally
                visits me
with the hide and engine
of a smoothly turning over tiger.

    So buses to Matala, port
      of dead heat, fried squids,
        glazed stone.

The hens squeal under the geranium leaves
little oodles all afternoon:
surprised by love, or by what
they can scuff out backwards,
          the sleepy spider
maker of sapphire girders.

4

The hero on the bow-bellied mountain
stands; a ruff of whispery
red gold haute coiffure
adds breadth to a whiplash neck.
You were Heracles in the morning
shadows, the first to call
dawn to the slippery surf and to
the drought stiff grass,
where you moved like a coin chieftain
        with few brains.

Now in his peignoir, stippled,
dappled, eyelids carved
like a monseigneur's out of hot
geranium, his side-eye
turned in a disk, as he scratches by;
and flutters, like a fish its gills
showing its whites.
He moves quietly
adding his oodles
           to those
of the others, quiet sounds
appropriate to a day
under the bow-bellied hills.

5

This same evening
two men and a girl in red
come with a truck and remove the hens
who trail their ignominious calls
upside down in rapid hands.
The cock is the last to go
tending his territory
in harried strides
                and scythe-tailed jumps,
letting the wives and chicks go first.

Close the shutters
            close the eyes

In these parts I hear
the shout against snakes
                no more

no more the annunciated
blue blossom
in stony Matala
in the dark of the morning.

Closed are my eyes.

> *In sea green shadows*
> *in dark waters*
> *the town sprats play*
> *upright, bobbing*
> *on their aquatic harpsichord.*

The beach of darlings

Behind the small cypresses
step the row of important girls.

Snakes climb their upper arms
their corselets offer up their breasts
to the god they spend all childish

passion to dance at her or his shrine.
Long hooped skirts
poise to a stop like tea-cozies.

Flouncy, bionic. Find them
at Wikipedia and the ancient sites.
Sure, they existed.

Grit and the pink marble lumps
of a palace gone aeons.
A windy foreshore, so the blind poet tells.

I wander as far as my own teenagers

hissing and buzzing
like little snakes and honey bees
jumping in the rock roses.

Wave my handkerchief,
not white, not black,
nobody any more to totter off a cliff

for a child lost, that's all done.

Sail on under plain calico,
goodbye my beach of darlings,
tired, sneaky, persistent sentiment,

old salt stiff,
hung out on the earth's curve.
Goodbye to that extraordinary sun.

PART IV

By the kitchen window

By the kitchen window
on the chair there's a basket,
in the basket, a box,
in the box a perfect egg,
the egg of the roc, the dodo's egg.
In the egg there's a yolk
huge as a rolled wave,
the bruise you'd get when
your lifelong horse you so love
upends its hind hoof
against your forehead
without end,
the horse you stroke and whisper to.
The yolk bursts never,
it remains black blue.
You are the eggshell, the crash barrier
and the truck is crashing, crashing.
You never break.

You must sit on the chair.
You must hold the basket.
On your lap you rock the nest,
two clutching hands at its ribs.
Don't touch the perfect egg,
the wearied mechanism of legends.
It comes from nowhere, everywhere.
You peer at what may be its oval
through the perspex side of the box:
hands in prayer, legs together,
black curls, cherry lips asleep;
the prince — you are the prince, of course.

You keep wondering:
Shall I open the box?
But the box is a glass cube.
No one opens the box.
Inside the mockery,
the blue black yolk,
inside the yolk
the nucleus:
impenetrable,
whatever is crashing around inside.

In the garden

There in the woods stand two
entwined aspens. I hear they are that pair,
Baucis and Philemon
long in the service of god, who chose
never to leave the other. Here
in the garden we sit before the
tea tray, eat chocolate biscuits,
one each, and talk of plants and birds and trees.
Your glowing face turns to me:
tell me. You want to hear everything,
that impossible menu.
I soufflé a life. My father
talks away on the phone by the door.
Two trees of life, not in the woods,
but in the garden.

Sun and trees

They are favourites of creation and
you planted them, and did you ever think
they're nearly as old as me?
Aren't we here together among our trees
and shall we discuss their many ways?
They have straighter backs, I admit.
They glow in your shrouded sun,
and so I collar its beams, aim them
at your silver Georgian teapot. This garden
and the lady of its walks are mine, I declare,
so before the others whisk you away

please attend your sun,
and on this straight crooked arm
walk as mistress through the glowing trees
to your inch by inch horizon,
the rim of your saucer,
the cup of your garden.

Hawthorns

The trees are hawthorn groves, rowans,
chestnuts, what does it matter,
signs of grief, sign of conscience.

An evil god of process laboured
and brought forth these good and
hopeful trees — the evil lies heavily

in your absence, and on a house so rich,
full to the brim, with carpets from the souks,
with filigree porcelain fisher-boys.

What long days they fish
from the mantelpiece, in their helpless nets,
what golden leaves.

Care giver

Sometimes I would lift her body
naked, bowed with bone disease,
to my shoulder, trying to free her

and my supine father from the icy
river water which made free
to cover their sleeping faces each

morning, before she could raise up
and put on the kettle for tea.
But then she would quail at me,

seeing me, now reversed, as a despot
ending their free life, free to
breathe, to swim… I understood her.

Truthfully I was superfluous, all
my presence was this dull defending,
to break the water from his eyes,

free her windpipe from grass and reeds.
In this skinny thin help at least
I lost my fame as troublemaker.

If my head burned in the bushes
her soft old skin wasn't reddened.
And so they lived on, in their lively river.

At the icy river

The icy river covered my father's eyes.
His body rose and lay back in my arms,
I carried him naked out of all disguise.

I felt him weighing, head and chest and thighs
like milk; his face was turned away and calm.
The icy river covered my father's eyes.

I carried him like an unexpected prize.
I tried to keep him safe and out of harm.
I carried him naked out of all disguise.

Over and over I struggled up a rise,
hoping to find some house or buried farm.
The icy river covered my father's eyes.

We slept in filthy kitchens under rotting skies,
his body a skin, a membrane, barely warm.
I carried it naked out of all disguise.

My father left my arms as I grew wise,
and back to the water all that time he swam.
I carried him naked out of all disguise.
The icy river covered my father's eyes.

A word

A word from the sweet old man
with the bald cranium who

places his long finger to his lip,
nurturing the guest who talks.

Mime and silence.
He sits in the room, feted,

taking his old birthday with
due dignity and a soft wit.

Everyone says, as they always do,
how, O how does he do it?

He forms his lips from my shelf,
the only place in the known world

where he and she,
like china figurines

so fragile to the duster's sigh,
might still be assured of a life.

A message of love

He left me a message of love.
— He left you a message,
shall I shout it, shall I save it?
— What message? — A message of love,
he left you a message of love.

Quite often he left me
a message, a message simply
of love, how little he had to add,
how little he needed to say
after leaving his love.

He left me a message of love.
I heard it many times and smiled
at the end of an evening out.
I'd missed him again, so I guessed,
and mostly you guessed

when I got the hoarse words
when you walked in and PLAY.
I wanted my bed and I said
I'm sure it's a message of love,
I'll bet it's a message of love.

But what could he say?
He was blind not as a bat,
he saw both the light and dark,
he spoke in the dark like a youth,
he left the message of love.

He lived in the dark and
he wanted the light which had
left him for good, so what he
would leave me was chanced
all the more, his message of love.

You called, do you want to listen?
as I trod up to bed, and
I called back, tomorrow tomorrow
and tomorrow I'll call him —
of course, he'll be pleased.

How I miss the light of his voice,
busy and nimble, and the same:
no need to ring back, please say
that her father rang, that he wishes
to leave her his love.

Moth

on my father's tenth anniversary, 03. 08.01

A moth ticking, persistent.
The fluorescent tube
hot, long, white overhead,
my head bent till twilight.

Summer outside, high summer.
It was on August third.
All still. A flutter
at the pulse of the throat.

Salt lick

I licked it up and kept it in,
closed my lips and sank my chin.

She lives away, in heaven or hell,
the one who never loved me well.

She must have lived because she's dead.
Jam and butter and a pinch of bread.

Old salt scar on old white skin,
such bitterness will do you in.

A drip of milk ran down my chin,
I licked it up and tucked it in.

Your eyes, not seen for a year

of my mother, at the geyser pool, Yellowstone Park

If my breath doesn't hold
where shall I be?

Will I slip down? When he gasps at the end
and goes down
will I empty out completely?

What breathes, Echinus,
and first stretches up
to scratch the sleeper's finger?

The accidental foot slip into the Sapphire Pool,
the Emerald Pool, the Chromatic, the Onyx,
the beautiful Morning Glory,
the Shield, the Oyster, the Necklace.
Here they are,
scalding, simmering,
searing away the rags,
the jewels of the body —
irrecoverable.

Your eyes were the blue Doublet pools,
not seen for a year.

I breathed in, or out,
two chilly hours, standing in wait.
Up rose the mill pond — Echinus!
The thorny, spiny old man of the spring.
The pool kept pulsing back,
round and round,
steaming white crocheted wavelets
 — the sea a long way away —
robing, unrobing his calcite ribs.

Then this far western sorceror
expired down his two thousand feet fall
of rock, gas, scald.

Each three hours he scratches the still water,
the show commences.

You were the fountain,
the gas scald, the upwelling, the sparkling.
Not seen for a year.

Your eyes were the dark blue pools,
unseen ever again.

How shall I breathe out?
How shall I step from the water's exquisite breath
if you, no longer and never again?

Creek

Pennsylvania. The clear creek
roars, mucky, spiky with broken trees.
Into the forest it dashes curdling arcs of foam.
Oak, ash, maple, sycamore
firing soft or hard gold-orange.
Secondary growth, but still
thick leaves and water din
hiding the silences,
deer, raccoon, rabbits.
Silence, astonished, awed even.
The year round. The day — again.
I thought, all my life through,
it couldn't come once.
I knew so: no, it cannot.

If you've crossed through this year,
You'll know the whole firecracker,
the burnt eyesight like red paper,
how suddenly it sucks down,
bangs you on flashing rocks,
bangs your head to drum you sensible,
the curdling descent,
have some sense: she's dead, he's dead,
all of you (you, them) extinguished underwater.

The piece of wood goes popping up for air.
Gulp some, dragged down again, roll, flounder,
begin to remember, but what?
From either side the hollows breathe out,
water on rock: forget —
for your own sake get across.

In the precincts

We're in the precincts now.
Where do I stand?
Which door do I stand at?
Which knocker, which handle

revolving like a symphony?
Which temple, since surely
I should tiptoe
— a sparrow, a priestess,

someone appointed
at some point: with such
an air of confidence —
In short, can I now be told,

know where I'm going?
Others thunder in.
This temple has an altar,
It's old Biddy's neatly

made bed, spotlessly
white crocheted altar lace,
what she gets for a life of disillusion:
the holy relentless.

Calm

There are the Scotch pines,
ink in the storm,
pink I scribbled like satin footmen,
I was trying my style
in the guttering chandeliers of stately evenings.
They grew up with me,
alternative brothers,
my family, solid and calm,
in the growing absence of angels they were mine.

Bare feet on my mother's green path
led to the little horizon,
a curly knuckle on the hand of the Weald;
there like a rude finger sprang up the obelisk
of Mad Jack Fuller, Squire
who after a lifelong binge
sat down on his stately dining-room chair
upright for good
in his graveyard pyramid.
Jack stays just so.
My good trees are calm.
I flew away, I had to.
They were a frieze of guttering wind-torn angels.

One should visit the family, the dead.
I pick up the yellow leaves of the tulip-tree
I sit on the bench under its huge limbs.
I look blind into the midday sun,
the ghosts barefoot on another ridge,
for a moment all tears.

After Murnau

Mirage
one summer hot as hell
— in Munich, in Murnau
where red ponies kicked the brown earth
where matron cows merrily
churned over the moon,
a time when joy
would kick up its unicorn heels,
run through green pastures.

A tall date palm
under which Mary sat,
her child shaded on her lap,
with running water at her feet,
everything to hand.
The desert stretches out,
the wilderness of lions
becomes her rampart,
loneliness become her
helpful convoy. Her child, herself,
their happy life ahead, in waiting, invincible.

You welcome her,
and so will I...
The lightning shoots like a stem
in the travelling sky
and here you are.
A tremulous thunder
— summer long of sickness,
how would you care for
the baby, everything, on your own?
I said, you, we can do this.

Everything, you wanted to repeat,
will be all right. Yes, oh yes,
if we have our say!

My god, one summer hot as hell,
loneliness her convoy —
The cow said in my thoughts
we will have our say!
The child in the shade under the date palm
the red earth, the moon perches
on the tree of the desert
for a while like a cluster of dates;
trips away, just the other day,
where did it go,
west, east, north, south,
a crescent moon stained
like a flower,
who could see it trembling
seen and lost in the day sky?

'pool of light'

for Mimi Khalvati

Without thinking, a moonlit flood,
white as a cherry-tree in jubilance.
Your mirror-tree refracted somehow

to a moon in full flood: this mirror-moon,
my quite misremembered dazzle,
stood in a garden, in a Highgate road.

But you, for whom your mirror-tree
flickered dark and light, and the room
kept a diary of that self,

you're there and gone, to your other rooms.
Also come gold, snow, lavender, amber…
Before, your grandmother, sugar-breaker,

morning maker of the sugar-bowl.
'Salaam, my daughter-lovely-as-the-moon.'
A childhood, a revolving house…

Your lines are your own silk routes,
tough, tramping your northern city;
myrrh; and kids' laughter, in cold air.

Now the room notes the 'acorn sea'.
And sun rises, and enters. Love writes
each room, each 'pool of light', from secrecy

to opened secrecy, dazzling, yours the gift.
Mistakes and all, I took it to my heart:
the snow-light on the bare ceiling,

its ruby heart, face of winter, face of summer,
watching how, not moon but love's sun shivers
to the peacock's spreading fan of poems

just as your tree, or mosaic in the street,
stood mirror, all that you saw and sang:
What is broken, what is made of it and sung,

the sweat of your bashful peacock of light,
the falling drop, your 'pool of light.'

Woman in the Moon

She hangs down her face,
her two rag arms,
caught in the glittering arms

of the crescent, can't hold
up their white hands
even with surprise

— why am I here,
dangling like Pierrot
in the cupboard between shows?

They open their palms
full of nothing beyond.

Lady shining with pain,
mouse in the moon's side,
round the curtain

creeps revolutionary time:
through the dark years and the light
pokes the glint of its eye,

lunatic and kindly,
rag bonnet and lace bonnet.
Round swishes the room.

Ultima Thule

In the suburbs of my wandering
I used to walk my dog by night.
I let him off the lead.
He quartered the district

sniffing for the half-open door.
The two of us, we never found it
before all darkness fell;
my dog trotted ahead.

For a time Ultima Thule
like a frost enveloped the house,
a white inrushing
so cold you couldn't breathe,

so hushed, you certainly
couldn't be a child,
cry for a dog, a mother dead,
the door jammed shut somewhere.

In the suburb of the bronze doors

1

Time clickety clicks through the fog
and we learn again to scrub these dull scenes

of expulsion, suffering, redemption
to their pitch perfect factory shine.

The last click comes! Ditching the polish,
we behold Sesame. Lo,

the dazzling doors,
like a lion's mouth at a beetle.

See them split wide, and Adam and Eve
& Pinchme, or just me,

we'll walk from the pensive allotment
where we dug at an ash garden

for all these ash years, returning at night
to the ash hotel room.

*

Some will take hoes, trugs of bulbs,
young plants, their roots dangling like foals.

Afterwards they'll reel off their wisdom, like
rhubarb, lilies, lanterns, winter pansies, rhubarb...

they planted them, they know the way.
Sesame is glossy like unwrapping a large lily bulb,

tonight she hops on the shut turnstile,
with a mystic tail

and the crowd will go again tomorrow
and everything will be more beautiful still.

2

What do I know?
As you do: the unweeded bed,
the broken hut, and around that
the clearing in the wood.

Each turning in the yellow-leaved wood,
rain pouring down, the banks treacherous
above the deer-grazed stream in the gloom,
always the same, the dance that has to
lower itself, then climb with eight arms.
The wood stands by a stream
or in the meadow, on the remote hill:
these are wild clearings.
Go on, say they are gardens.

Whether we lie this side or that
of the superannuated scenes,
the gross old whitebeard lasered down from Mars,
the marchpast of the thousand invented child saints —
at a pindrop, often still,
I seem to myself to shrivel,
a dead bee case, against your will
(you are so scared) —

The yellow layered sodden leaves, always
remembered, the prayers, a child's factory,
a secretive never stopping production line:
lemon leaves, the drops of rain
on the wild and jealous sweets of the wood,
poison prayers, curses poured on wilder poison,
each curse fruiting the rot beneath,
the lot abandoned long past.

Slithery grief,
a clearing to no better.
I and Pinchme, still we garden the wood.
we sit in our hut,
our valuable carcase of honey.

*

And whether we even met Sesame,
whether we salted the mystic tail,
I doubt. Her warblings, her chimes,
the cranks of the doors backsliding
on rusted runners — not worth a dime.
A desperate moonshine of what
once may have come before.
Was it a real grove or garden
of what was once mine?

3

I live as you do.
One morning I shake up joy.
Doors are half open, half closed.
I shake it up in its jar on the shelf,
like a squall over the bed
and within the constrictions given
to the hut dwellers (slivered time, space),
out bursts fire from our town of fireworks,
wood of windflowers, pleides.
As for the guards at the doorpost:
we loop, we hopscotch time,
our spread wings are inky fingers,
bright ever hope of entry,
spiralling, rolling above the houses
and the lights stuck at dark.

                Down down
clowns on the prowl, hop hop
by tunnel by claw after all
                      into a garden
beyond the long woods of our shadows.

The Garden of Earthly Delights

for Carolyn Trant

1

I am the child of a bird
dark robin's child
I am the child of the fruit

A hoopoe, yellow or blue
thumbs a berry
in the stab of a beak,
looks after me sternly

Clone of a jay
brings me a berry
as big as my head

We fruit in the beaks
and the branches of a garden
without end
that never had a gate,
never a seed scattered,
a hand on a spade

In the garden
what is wrong is put right,
our bodies fruit with bodies,
our bodies dive and swim

I carry a fish for my pride
for my second head

A bird is my head
is the eye that thinks and winks

Nothing is right so
nothing is wrong
in the labyrinthine fruits
of the garden of delight —

2

We crawl, throstlings
into summer's caves,
into the flesh of pomegranates,
strawberries, burst translucent
beads of the wild rose,
gift of our wicked nurses
owl, jay, rat, mouse —

I talk my nonsense
to the owl's surprise
She likes my jokes, bird
of thought, her eye
is a dark home

We crawl into our flesh
Silly, it doesn't quite work

I talk to our mouths,
to our backsides
All is one and one is all
Every mouth is wrong
and every mouth is right

3

A bird stoops to stab me
I crawl into my flesh
Flesh swallows me,
swallows you —

Each bird bends
its beady eyes to love

comical love, that clown,
buffoon of buttocks and breasts

I gawp at your head
You squint through the hole
Delight is wholly a garden,
holy fruit, the holes in fruit,
ripe, rotting — ever the
fruit runs riot, and ripens —
Anyone can squirm through,
you, me and Sesame —

Open wide — what
word or womb or which wide?

A family joke,
a joke of leaves and birds

Faces of innocence
and alabaster arses
we're all here
happy as blue jays
green as woodpeckers

Sharp as the point of flight

All is one is one and one is all
every mouth is wrong
and every mouth is right —

4

Your foot sticks through
the rind, my head pops out
Nothing's a surprise,
what's wrong is right

Swap me a bird head
for two wagging feet

Join the parade, canter, crawl,
what's wrong is best of all

ride inside a husk, a haw, a hip,
dig where your hands like,
you'll find the talking food

and juice is full of running words
and words are flesh
are leaf, belief,
whichever way you fall

Sentences are branch and arm
Forest is word, flesh, beak, desire
Berries are my castle

Whatever's wrong is right
and winter's gone for good
and gone to bad
Winter cannot wax
as red as autumn berries

The mouths of birds,
mountainous birds, long-legged,
are crammed with all I need

just what I need,
to live in an orange

to gush in the fountain
that never dries, never dies

5

I dive into my life,
water falls around my black skin
glossy as an elderberry

in the bird harvest
in the zenith
sloshing in the pool
I'm sure I'll live forever

I'm the harvest of birds,
their round eyes spot us,
hanging, falling. We are
the bird who spots the
round, the lozenge, the hip, haw,
the blueberry rolling —

We creep, we jostle
to our fleshy dens
into our fleshpots
forever and amen

In then out
stick in your head
stick out your foot
one foot in, two heads out

Not a foot wrong
and all is right
What's wrong is best foot first,
pure delight
Splosh in, you can't go right
or wrong, you and I —
Gush of delight!

6

O fierce bird
stab me, guard me
so I never die

The spurt of the fountain —
Never dry up, never die
I'm sure I'll never grow old

I am the fool
of the comic garden

I'm the fool and the food,
the child in the belly of the fruit
My mother's the bird of desire

Nothing is right
and nothing is wrong
forever and ever and ever
in the garden of earthly delights.

Grandchild

I spoil my lovely grandchild.
a two year old who cajoles
to be carried in shops, and nibbles my earring,
murmuring,
her fingers prancing my necklace.

I rock her
as my mother had rocked my own daughter
as a young baby crying,
demonstrating with serenity
how to soothe a strange infant
— By the way I knew nothing.
when my own child was born, nothing —

Born of fear
into moments and hours of unusual joy.
Time was a bird. Could it be
I began ignorant of her song
though of her beauty, never?
For she was Artemis,
swift and strong-legged,
brave and black-curled, like the one
who threw and tied snakes together.
Weapons… like patience, like courage.

The lovely baby of my child,
two years old,
comical…
I still know little of sweet Artemis,
grandchild, deep blue eyed, charmer,
stroker of earrings.

Sorry Go Round

I heard of the garden of earthly delights.
Hard times, how to get in?
I tried every which way
memory, satire, strict conformity with the age,
sarcasm, false moustache, stolen identity.
I was returned each night
to my ash hotel room.
Occasionally a bunch of prize gladioli.
I was a dance in the inquisitor's
long reach, sometimes the flagellant,
other times wrecking hope,
wide-eyed good-natured hope.
Pity my state. (O good friends!)

Wide-eyed hope one day
took pity, I can't work out why,
some kindness, some answer.
I found myself in the pack again,
fighting to get over, to ram
through, who knows, to sneak under.
Unexpectedly hope glossed itself
as a fat black raven.
How I remembered their somersaults
over the mountainsides,
tumblers, entertainers,
sombre as clerics
and cleverer.
No garden of Eden, Fall, serpent,
apple, Eve, bliss, damnation,
the promise of the hairy bosom of Abraham.
Not really. I wanted my mother.
Not really but anyway not Abraham.

One day the raven
lifted me up and flew me
in a single trice
over the bronze gates
which showed no sign of wear and tear
at the endless ambuscade
I have related
and which I joined so fiercely for years.
Bang, bang, but nothing fell down
or was even dented.
And there I was, and there
I could not be.

But earlier I grew there
that part of me in gladness,
part of me, a half woman in joy.
Take me with you when you
also go there.

I feel like a remnant
that busily fretfully writes:
take me with you!
Why should strangers rescue strangers?

The raven's gaze,
impervious to all but a mouse —
a flicker soon to be gone —
then blank itself —
my eyes rolling down straight slopes of scree
seeing nothing, going nowhere —
I cried to that raven in its tumbling
down, going down,
take me with you,
find me where you know I am,
in that thing called joy.

I take pictures of butterflies
Common Blue, uncommon as planets
Gatekeeper, Copper, Meadow Brown;
I'm crouching and groaning
on sore legs, sore bum,
I come back from the fields
with my box aflutter
with gauzy dustings of hope.
I don't know what to do with hope.
I dust them all to you.

All my life people have told me
joy, hope, faith, hope and charity,
they're all there inside you —
just a matter of identity, recognition,
liberation, empowerment, trying,
obeying, subverting, anything really.
Who knows beyond themselves?
I hurt, I beaver away, I am:
That's the ticket. Hope has no ticket,
you can't catch hope to anywhere.

Like a raven it lives
on the edge of a tall cliff,
the sort near here where people
go to die. But hope soars
and dives comfortably,
in its time, in its state.
So I will sing to hope,
who lives on a terrible cliff
rearing up
in the garden of joy.

Acknowledgments

Thanks are due to the editors of the following publications, where some of these poems first appeared:

Agenda, Ambit, Artemis, Children of Albion, The London Magazine, Parvenu Press, the Morning Star, The North, Poetry Review, Poetry Wales, Poetry and Audience, Poetry South East 2010, Poetry Salzburg Review, The Rialto, Resurgence, Stand, and *Tabla*.

Other poems were first published in EA Markham (ed) *Plant Care: a Festschrift for Mimi Khalvati* (2004), Eva Salzman and Amy Wack (eds) *Women's Work: Modern Women Poets Writing in English* (2008), Michael Hulse (ed) *The King's Lynn Silver Folio: Poems for Tony Ellis* (2009) and Jeremy Page (ed) *Poems from the Old Hill: a Lewes Anthology* (2012).

'The Garden of Earthly Delights' was first published with collagraphs by Carolyn Trant in *The Garden of Earthly Delights: a Response to Bosch* (2003).

Other poetry books by Judith Kazantzis

Minefield
(Sidgwick And Jackson, 1977)

The Wicked Queen
(Sidgwick And Jackson, 1980)

Touch Papers
(with Michele Roberts And Michelene Wandor,
Allison And Busby, 1982)

Let's Pretend
(Virago, 1984)

Flame Tree
(Methuen, 1988)

A Poem for Guatemala
(Greville, 1988)

The Florida Swamps
(Oasis, 1990)

The Rabbit Magician Plate
(Sinclair Stevenson, 1992)

Selected Poems 1977-1992
(Sinclair Stevenson, 1995)

Swimming Through The Grand Hotel
(Enitharmon, 1997)

The Odysseus Poems: Fictions on The Odyssey Of Homer
(Cargo, 1999)

Just After Midnight
(Enitharmon, 2004)

Mad King George on Tom Paine
(The Tom Paine Press, 2009)

Clickety Clackety, Eight Nursery Nasties
(Nuts in May, 2012)